DIAMONDS FROM THE ROUGH

Diamonds From The Rough
by Bill Corum

www.prisonpowerministries.org

Published by Power Publishing
PO Box 281
Lone Jack, MO 64070-0281

Edited by Bill and Debbie Corum

Cover design and layout by Kevin Williamson
www.kevinwilliamsondesign.com

Scripture quotations in this book are from the following Bible versions:

ISBN 978-0-9895249-9-5

Printed in the United States of America

DEDICATION

This book is dedicated to all the men and women who are living behind razor-wire fences, gun towers, and high walls. And to those who have been there and are now on the outside.

The Bible says, The Lord . . . is patient with you, not wanting anyone to perish but everyone to come to repentance (II Peter 3:9).

ABOUT *DIAMONDS FROM THE ROUGH*

This book you are holding in your hands is about nine of my personal friends. I consider them to be diamonds. Diamonds are considered precious gems— "the most prized of all gems" to be specific. Natural diamonds are formed over time under extreme pressure and heat. Expert diamond cutters then use their knowledge and skill to cut, polish, and make them into beautiful, multi-faceted gems.

My original thought was to title this book Diamonds In The Rough. Nothing could be further from the truth. These nine indeed came from the darkest places on the earth. They began their journey with Christ *in the rough.* Their lives took shape through great trials, heat, and under tremendous pressures. God—the expert jeweler—then cut (pruned) and polished my friends into the beautiful, precious gems they are today. They agree that had His hand not been upon them, they would still be very much in the rough. Praise God, that is no longer the case. They yielded their lives to Christ and followed Him. As a result, their stories were forever changed. Thus, the name *Diamonds From The Rough*.

When you read their stories, you'll see that they have two things in common—they went after Jesus with the same energy that they went after whatever got them locked up. They also long for others to discover that same peace and joy they have found in Jesus.

If you give God permission, He will begin the process of turning you also into a precious gem. He wants to be your best friend. He is a good, good Father and only has the best in store for you.

In HIS grip,

Bill Corum

II Corinthians 5:17

FOREWORD

BY BILL CORUM

Decades ago, when I returned home from doing a prison weekend, my wife asked me how it went. I told her that it was wonderful. More than wonderful. "I didn't want to come home." She knows I have a call from God to do prison ministry. Still, hearing me say that didn't sit so well.

"I didn't mean it that way, honey," I explained. "I just meant it was so good, that I want to die of a heart attack in a prison telling prisoners how Jesus changed me."

Debbie answered with, "Please don't say that. The Bible says we speak life or death with our tongues. It says we eat the fruit of our lips."

"Okay, I'm sorry. How's this? I want to die of a heart attack in a prison, telling inmates how Jesus changed me when I'm ninety-five."

She said that would be okay.

A friend wisely said, "Every heart has an expiration date." Only God knows when mine is. If He wills me to live to age ninety-five, then I have eighteen more years as of this writing. During which time, I plan to reach as many with the Good News of the Gospel as possible. One way is through books. Books can reach more people than I ever could speaking in person. My plan is to continue writing and publishing as many life-changing books as possible and getting them into prisons before I go to be with the Lord.

Perhaps you've already enjoyed reading: *The Ultimate Pardon* or *Nuggets of Gold by 12 Ex-Cons*. If so, I have good news for you—there are more books coming.

Diamonds From The Rough excites me because I know the impact success stories can have on people. Especially stories of those that society writes off as losers, saying they will never change or amount to anything.

I was once one of those losers. When I came to the Lord in 1983, I was facing possibly going back to prison for the rest of my life. What I needed was hope that I could change. I found that hope in Jesus and in the Bible—and in reading stories of reformed gangsters, drug addicts, alcoholics, dealers, and killers. Those men and women had been just as messed up as I was, yet they turned their lives completely around. They were now living successfully without looking over their shoulders at every turn. I wanted that kind of success more than anything. So, I read, and read, and read. The more I read, the more hope I received. I figured if they could change by trusting in God, so could I.

This year 2021 makes my thirty-eighth year of salvation and my thirty-third year in prison ministry. I'd say my life was indeed changed by trusting in God.

I meet inmates across the country that come up to me and say, "Bill, I tried God and He didn't work." I look them in the eye and say, "He didn't work the way you tried Him." If you try God your way, He will never work. If you try Him His way, He will always work. His way is total surrender, giving everything to Him.

If you've tried and failed, it's okay. You haven't lost unless you quit. If you don't quit, God won't quit. Go with God my friends and enjoy this book. It was written for YOU.

Blessings my friends as you read this book.

TABLE OF CONTENTS

ANY DAY NOW

JOE NARVAIS

MY NAME IS JOE NARVAIS. My number is 386644. If you are familiar with the Texas prison system, you'll know by my number that I've been around a while. The things I was involved in brought a lot of hurt to people and families. They were bad enough that the state of Texas took away my freedom for over twenty-five years. I have a bunch of war stories I could tell you, but I won't. I *will* tell you a few of the things I was involved in, so you realize the miracle that has happened in my life.

My journey began at a young age with the influence of those around me. Although my mom was a Christian and a prayer warrior, my dad was the one everyone looked up to because he was in prison. Visiting him in prison was normal. Conversations about prison were also considered normal. I remember the pride in my grandfather's eyes when he told the many stories of his son's past crimes and violence. He spoke of him with deep respect, describing him as someone strong, tough, crazy. "Your dad is 'machine'", he'd say to me. Like a machine, he was without emotion, a soldier willing to do whatever was necessary. There was no hesitation or remorse.

I admired my dad for that. I wanted him to one day be as proud of me as his father was of him. I considered prison a part of life, something everyone must go through to become a man. In my teen years, I spoke of prison regularly to my neighborhood friends, even considered their dads to be weak because they hadn't done time. I was convinced I was doing myself and my friends a favor by getting us *prison ready*. "You can't get away with that in prison," I'd tell them, implementing prison rules and discipline into our daily routines. Violence was the normal way to solve problems. At the time, it was the only way of life.

Add to that, my mindset of no fear of the law and a desire to benefit financially, and it didn't take me long to begin my life of crime. At age fifteen, I started stealing cars and selling them to my uncles who owned body shops. They were hooked on heroin and sometimes burned me on paying for the cars. So, one day I stole a jeep and headed to Mexico where I traded it for drugs. I became a young hustler with people stealing cars for me, which I in turn traded for drugs in Mexico. Stealing and selling cars eventually led me to a buyer from Mexico. Liking the way I carried myself, he set me up in the drug business. My brother, who was a biker, also wanted to sell cocaine, so I started him and my uncles selling dope for me. Instead of graduating from high school, I got my diploma from the streets. I was able to get anything, anytime. I thought I was King Kong, can't go wrong. Then BAM!!

By age nineteen, I was on my way to college in the big house (penitentiary), charged with possession of heroin and aggravated assault with an axe hammer on two men. It was my first time down. But I was prepared to face my eight-year sentence with the same violence and no-fear attitude that had gained me respect on the streets. I learned even more about hustling, fighting, and making money while living the convict life. Four years later, I made parole.

My connections in Mexico bought me a plane ticket and I was right back in business. It was as though I had never left. There was little time to spend with my mother, father, and young son. I started making people sell my product only. If I caught them selling anyone else's drugs, they got robbed and set on fire. Things were going well. For two years, I was "The Man". Then BAM!!

My next four-year bit was on dope charges. This was my second trip back and I was still doing the same things. Hustling, fighting, living up to my reputation led me to serve all of that sentence.

When I hit the streets again, I was angrier, more violent and vengeful. I hadn't learned a thing. So much time had been lost! I felt the state owed me something for locking me up. But fast life leads to fast time.

My third trip back to prison was different. I was to serve my ten-year sentence at "The Ham" (as everyone called it) with its gun towers and razor wire—far from home, and family, and my daughter who was now on the way. Eastham Unit was the prison's actual name. We called it "The House of Pain" because of the violence. The October 6, 1986 issue of *Newsweek* magazine described Eastham as "the most dangerous prison in America". Knifings and beatings were common. Guards were vicious and played both ends of the game. I saw old men die and young men get killed there. It had earned its reputation.

Things happened at The Ham that I won't write about. I'll just say that in the six years I spent behind those walls, my heart became meaner and harder. More deeply scarred. I was good at hustling on the streets, so became just as good hustling and making money on the inside. Eastham became my home away from home. I knew how to survive in the Department of Corrections. I was now a convict, not an inmate.

When I made parole, I was more careful. I learned to pace myself. Started a relationship with my son and daughter, which built my mom's hopes that her prayers were finally working. I was making money, buying cars and houses, spending time on the lowrider scene. Some of the seven cars I owned ended up in *Lowrider* magazine.

During that time, I also met a beautiful young girl. We moved in together. She liked traveling with me to car shows and loved my lifestyle and the way people respected me. My family was comfortable and happy. She was happy. Everything was good. But I was living a double life. Because I never respected the law or feared it, I never stopped breaking it. Many of you reading this can relate. I figured nothing could stop me this time. I was making lots of money, had nice cars . . . and my girl. I lived it up for nearly two years. Then BAM!!

This time was not like the others. As a repeat offender caught with a significant number of drugs, I was looking at two life sentences. My out date on the first case was 99/99/9999. The second was also 99/99/9999. That was Texas' way of saying, "Never!" I was told I would die in prison.

This left me with no hope. Figuring I had nothing to lose, I became even more dangerous. I needed to get myself ready for being 'machine'. No weakness. No doing time with a girl. As soon as my girl was able to come see me, I told her, "Don't ever come back." She said she loved me. I told her, "I can't do time with a woman. Don't come back." From then on, my only visitors were my kids and family. I met my grandkids during visitation. I lost my dad while I was behind bars. This was my life.

I hustled and lived like a convict. My hurt turned to anger in order for me to survive. If you're reading this from prison, you know convict life comes with consequences. My nothing-to-lose attitude landed me in and out of the hole over the years. One time while in the hole, I was thinking about Jesus. Since I was raised Catholic, I knew about Jesus but didn't have a relationship with Him. I started praying and all of a sudden started speaking in tongues. The devil told me I had finally lost my mind. I said, "Jesus, if this is not of you, then take it away." I opened the Bible, and there it was—a scripture about tongues.

When I got out of the hole, I went to the yard to collect on some store a homeboy owed me. There, on the yard, a man was speaking about God. He'd also had two life sentences but was now free and speaking in prisons. It piqued my interest. I tried to listen despite my homeboy telling me not to.

When the service ended, I went up to the man and asked, "Who's your lawyer that got you out with two life sentences?"

He said, "Jesus."

"No, that's not what I mean. Who's your lawyer? What's his name?"

"Jesus got me out," he answered. "When you getting out?"

I didn't think he understood what I was asking, and I *sure* didn't understand what he was saying. I told him, "I got two life sentences. My out date is 99/99/9999. And when I finish that one, I have another one. I'm never gettin' out."

"Don't speak negative," he said. "Out of your mouth flow blessings and curses. You need to start speaking positive and believe God for a miracle. Start saying, 'Any Day Now'. You gotta have faith. Claim a date."

My mom always told me I needed to have faith. Maybe this guy was right because what he said was making sense. I forgot all about the coffee I came to the yard for.

Me finally *getting it* must've shown on my face, because the guy then said, "Now . . . when're you getting out?"

"Any day now, fool," I answered. That's what I called everyone back then. I was serious. I started saying, "Any day now" over and over. I told my mom to join me in claiming that I was getting out any day now. I said it, and said it, and said it hundreds of times a day.

Thirteen years and eight months into my sentence, I was paroled. But I had been free in my heart for years. I got out of prison June 2006 and am on life-time parole. In March 2018, my reporting changed from once a month to once a year.

God did it. He released me from prison in my mind, and later opened the doors for my physical freedom. No more shortcuts. No lies. I found freedom through Jesus. I tell men in prison that just saying those three words, "Any day now", will not get you out of prison. You have to live a life of no compromise, totally sold out and surrendered to God. God gave us His very best in His Son, Jesus. We can choose to give Jesus our very best. God knows none of us are perfect. That's why He gave His Son for our sins.

My dad was proud of me for the wrong reasons. Though he died, I know he knows who I am now. My son later followed in my footsteps and went to prison. I had taught him indirectly to do wrong. I'm not proud of that. It was painful seeing him behind glass because I knew the real way to be free.

Today, my son and I work together in our own business. I am close to my kids and grandkids. I have a great church family, people who love me and support me. My mother, who never gave up on me, gets a visit from me every day in her home. And the most exciting part of this whole God story? That good-looking girl who liked the show cars, the lifestyle, and the money I flashed around as a drug kingpin—that same girl I told to never come back because I couldn't do time with a woman—is now my wife. And my very best friend in this world. We go into jails and prisons together and tell of the loving and forgiving Father we both serve. I share my Any Day Now story and have actually seen God work in prisoners' lives like He did in mine. Only an awesome God can do all that!

We must understand how much our lives influence our families—our children, even nephews, nieces, and cousins. When we do time, so does our family. We lead by example. When we make a change in our lives, it's not just for us. It's for them. And for others we meet along the way.

If you want true change, there is one thing you must know. You cannot and will not be able to live right without God's help. Man may not be willing to forgive us of our past mistakes, but the Lord Jesus will. He is alive and will totally forgive us.

Over 2000 years ago, Jesus died on an old, rugged cross. All of your sins and my sins were nailed to that cross with Him. He was buried, and on the third day rose from the dead so you and I could receive forgiveness and life everlasting. *That if thou shalt confess with thy mouth the Lord Jesus, and shalt believe in thine heart that God hath raised Him from the dead, thou shalt be saved* (Romans 10:9).

Your Any Day Now begins right now when you ask Him to come into your heart and take control of your life. Ask Him to fill you with His Holy Spirit, Who will give you power to resist temptation and help you understand the Bible when you read it. Pray now and start your new walk with him.

When is your ANY DAY NOW coming?

Contact Information:
Joe Narvais
Cross to Freedom
PO Box 1131
Lubbock TX 79408

BEAUTY FOR ASHES

ROBIN LINDSAY

How does a woman go from being a pillar within her family, a respected member of society, and having an exciting career as a flight attendant—to a desperate life of drug addiction that led to jail and eventually to prison? Such a drastic transition in such a short period of time wasn't easy. But every drastic choice I made brought a drastic consequence.

My family and friends were in disbelief. They were devastated. I was the oldest of five children, raised by a young teen mother, my grandmother, and my aunts. Our household was well-fed, well-dressed, and well-loved in spite of having very little money. A day did not go by without someone saying, "I love you." It also wasn't uncommon to hear comments like: "Robin is an excellent student", "She is so well-behaved", "We never have to spank her", "She takes good care of her brothers and sister", and "What would we do without Robin?". I was the good kid. And because I wanted to maintain their opinion of me, I was careful—to a fault. That is, until I found a place where I thought I actually fit in . . . a place where I didn't have to *be* anything.

In high school, I started smoking weed, drank a little, and found that I liked to party. However, my circle of friends and I wouldn't even talk to you if you did hard drugs or got into trouble. At this point in time, I knew of no one other than my dad (living in a different city), who had ever been in jail.

My introduction to cocaine came at age twenty-seven—on my birthday, in fact. I had just moved from New York to the Midwest, where I worked as a flight attendant with an airline. The guy I was dating came from a family of high-rolling dope dealers. By the time I realized this, it was too late to change course; I was already in too deep with him and super intrigued by his lifestyle and the crowd he associated with. At their lavish parties, I was treated like a princess. Not only had I never met the likes of them, they had also never met the likes of me—a kind, beautiful, sweet, naïve girl from Topeka. They were the types I had only seen in movies: real pimps, hustlers, gangsters, and call girls. Their homes and cars were beautiful. Although stacks and stacks of money and trash bags full of dope were always available, none of them actually used the drugs they sold. I was given access to anything I wanted.

This life became increasingly attractive to me. In between flights, I would hang out with them, distancing myself more and more from my family, and from my best friend and roommate. She knew something was different about me and I could tell she didn't approve. So, I kept her as separate from my other life as I could.

One particular night at a club while I was on the dance floor with my boyfriend, his cousin handed me a package and said, "Happy birthday." When the song ended, I went to the bathroom and discovered that my mysterious gift was a hefty package of powder cocaine. When I told my boyfriend, his face lit up. That's when I found out that he was experienced at getting high on cocaine. I also learned that he was on the run from California for a crime he committed while he was high. The course of my life changed right then and there. He taught me the proper way to snort it and I was hooked. Night turned to daylight and I was still awake, snorting cocaine. I snorted it clear into the next day. My new *friends* made it available to me anytime I wanted more but made it clear that if I ever started smoking it, we would no longer be cool as friends. I would have to pay for it from that point on.

I began taking cocaine on trips with me and couldn't wait to get back home to my hangout. This went on for about six months. A woman came every two weeks or so with her velvet bags and glass pipes with flowers painted on them. She was a doctor. Her hair and clothes were immaculate; she wore diamonds and drove a corvette. I always watched her cook and smoke cocaine while I stayed true to my friends and still snorted it. When she asked me to try it, I hesitated. But what could it hurt? After all—look at her! Right? I went ahead and gave it a try. Thirty days later, I was in treatment, referred there by the airline union if I wanted to keep my job. I hadn't shown up at work much since I took that first hit off the pipe.

It may sound like I've glamorized this lifestyle that nearly killed me, but it was presented to me as a tempting gift-wrapped package. So, when I got out of treatment, I opened up that package again.

My former circle of friends no longer wanted me around. So, I moved back home, lost my job with the airline, and started writing checks out of my empty bank account. What would have been a misdemeanor, quickly turned to felonies. For about three-weeks straight, I traveled from city to city, writing checks for merchandise to sell to the drug dealers. Anything they ordered I would go get. I had a fairly easy time passing checks because I talked and dressed the part. I learned this from working retail. Before I knew it, I had racked up close to twenty-thousand dollars in bad checks out of my account. I never imagined I'd have to go to jail someday for this. Surely someone would rescue me.

One of my dope dealers thought we would make a great team. He asked me to drop the guy who introduced me to cocaine and move in with him—under one condition: I had to stop doing whatever I was doing to get merchandise to sell. There was no need for it now. So, I stopped writing checks and became his companion as he sold kilos of crack cocaine across the state.

One day, a close policeman friend contacted him and said, "Hey man, did you know your girl is on the Kansas Most Wanted?" He told him that they would eventually catch him while looking for me or catch me while looking for him. My first arrest came during a drug raid not long afterward. No one was charged, and they did not detain me for the checks. A few months later, cops surrounded my mother's house because they got word that my boyfriend was armed and dangerous. They had five felony warrants for me from five different counties. My mother cried as they brought me, handcuffed, out of her basement where I'd been hiding between two mattresses.

I spent the next several years in and out of jails, courts, treatment centers, halfway houses, oxford houses, churches, NA/AA, psychiatrists, and countless dope houses. In the midst of it all, I saw several glimpses of hope; they seemed to be connected to listening to or reading about God. Every time I was in treatment or a facility, I got into the Word, went to Bible studies, reached out to family and friends who went to church and said, "Hey, look at me! I am doing it too. I'm done using drugs; this time is different."

I began praying and practicing some of the principles I learned in the Bible. Yet, I was missing something. I never quite understood what it was they felt when they spoke about God. For the life of me, I couldn't figure it out. There was this certain light/glow in their smiles, a tone to their voices when they spoke of Him. I was seeking God because I wanted what they had, and they said they got it from God.

I believed God's Jeremiah 29:11 plan was in place, that it was a good plan, and that it would give me hope. *For I know the plans I have for you, declares the Lord, plans to prosper you, and not to harm you, plans to give you hope and a future.* I was willing to do *almost* anything to get it. I saw His miraculous hand at work clear back to when I first began seeking Him. But there were areas I struggled to give up. I lacked complete trust in His promises. Back then, doctors told me I had less than 10% chance of ever carrying a child to birth. I told God I'd never use drugs again if He would allow me to have a child. He did it instantly. I became pregnant and gave birth to my daughter (who is almost twenty-five at the time of this writing).

I continued to seek Him but kept using and going in and out of treatment and jails. My last time in prison (2004–2005), God gave me a major breakthrough. During a church service, I received an awakening. This was my first real taste of transformation for myself. It changed my heart. I read nothing but the Word and books pertaining to God. Violent and smutty books from the library no longer drew me. I was peaceful in prison. Others asked me to pray for them.

I also began to believe a prophetic word I'd received at age eighteen. The lady told me I had an anointing that God would use in His Kingdom. She said others would see this anointing all over me when they met me. Because I had no idea what she was talking about, I continued wandering in the wilderness a few more years, but still under God's protection. He was saving me all along, protecting me from harm, and sending people and circumstances to help accomplish this. Not once in my life, was I ever hit or spanked. I'd never had a fight, been raped, or physically harmed. I have been in groups with other women who experienced all of the above, and the amazing thing was that we *all* had the same emotions, and hurt, and the need for God in our lives.

Finally in 2012, while being jailed in county for the last time, I asked God to help. "Just help, Lord." I couldn't do it anymore. "Show me how to find You and stay this time." I had prayed this type of prayer a hundred times before, so I didn't even believe it myself. I figured God didn't believe me either.

But during those thirty days in county, I went to every Bible study they brought in. I also never called my PO to see if I could get out. In fact, the very day I was to go to court to decide if I'd be sentenced or released, I ordered commissary. This time I had truly surrendered to God. And He knew it.

I got out of jail, got a job (still working the same job today), joined a church, and got involved with helping others. I gave up my old running buddies and stayed as consistent as I could with the things God gave me to do. I believe with all my heart that God wanted me to know what my assignment was. So, He sent a special someone to help me carry this out. Spencer Lindsay was starting a ministry called Working Men of Christ (WMOC). Through him, I became a mentor with Kansas Department of Corrections, helped implement his first women's discipleship home, the House of Ruth.

Spencer and I are now married, my daughter graduated from college in May of 2019, I have a beautiful five-year-old granddaughter, and I've been free from drugs alcohol and crime for eight-and-a-half years!

When I don't know what to do—I go to God. When I don't know when—I wait on God. When I don't know why—I trust God. God is in control. Philippians 2:13 helps me remember that. *For God is working in you, giving you the desire and the power to do what pleases him.* God is working in me and through me to get His will done. I continue to be in awe of how He turns me around when I lose my way. Today when I smile, it is a genuine Spirit-led smile that comes from that same place I'd seen and longed for in others so many years ago.

Contact Information:
CrossRoads Restoration, Inc
Attn. Robin Lindsay
2010 NW Logan
Topeka KS 66608
Robin@crossroadsrestoration.org

GOOD OLE COUNTRY BOY (AKA DANO)

DAN BRISBIN

I STARTED MY JOURNEY OF DRUG ADDICTION, cops, jail, prison (and all that comes with), in the early 90's. It took me down a path I never dreamed I would travel.

I married young, bought a little farm in the country. By the time I reached the age of thirty, I was raising four children and by all appearances had my life together. I will spare you the details, except that I became sick with a disease which I was told had no cure. Within a year, I was pretty much bed ridden. One day while lying in bed, a friend came by and said, "I don't know if this will help, but this gives me a lot of energy". He cut out a big line of crank and offered it to me. I had experimented with pot and pills, drinking, and etc. in my teen years, but nothing like this. "Energy" was not even close to what I felt when his dope hit my system. For the first time in months, I was up and running. I decided right then and there that this wonder drug was for me.

I discovered real soon that I couldn't afford to keep buying it. So, I learned to make it. Which led to my addiction to money, which led to another discovery—easy accessibility to hookers because I had money. In the meantime, I lost my farm, my wife of eighteen years, and my children.

In just a few short years, I found myself not able to leave my driveway without being chased or arrested by the cops. That landed me in jail often. All the while, the dope had me by the throat and wouldn't let me go. I packed a pistol everywhere I went, kicked in doors of people owing me money. One guy who ripped me off, got scared when he heard I was coming for him. He waited in the street with a .22 rifle. As I drove toward him, he shot me through the windshield and ran back into his house. I floored it. My car went through his garage door and out the back wall into the next street. Thankfully, my windshield slowed the bullet enough that it only went into my shoulder about a half inch. I pulled it out and went home to heal. My money anonymously materialized the next day.

In one of my stays in county jail, there was this big guy. A bully. Because we were in a small town, most cellmates were scared of him. Two things make me mad—fear and bullies. So, one day on the yard I found a small garter snake and figured it would be a good idea to bully the bully, to see fear on his face for a change. My idea worked well. Everyone laughed their heads off—including myself—until he hit me. The fight was on. He was tougher than I thought. Whatever happened to bullies being cowards? After we'd fought for a while and were both pretty bloody, he ended up on his back with me on top of him on my back. He had me all but choked out. I knew it was about over for ole Dano! *Until* he began telling me in my ear what he planned to do to my lifeless body when I passed out. I'll tell you one thing for sure—you're better off hacking me off than scaring me. All I could see of him was his right eye, so I started banging away at that one eyeball with the elbow of my free arm. I didn't stop until I felt him go limp. He was a mess. His cheekbone was broken, and his eyeball hung out of his head. He told someone later that it felt like something bit his eye out. So naturally, a friend of mine gladly tattooed on my elbow, an eyeball with teeth biting it.

One day, about a mile from home on a gravel road, I noticed the cherries on top of a cop car sticking up above the brush at the cross-road ahead (he thought he was well hidden). I pulled over and hit the woods running. The cop took out after me on foot through the field, hollering for me to stop. I ran into a big gulley thinking I might ditch him there. Between being up for days, a possible drug overdose, *and* the adrenaline rush, I was running out of steam. I decided to hide under a big rose bush and wait him out. This was my steep learning curve to never stop running until outside of their jurisdiction. Of all things, I fell asleep or passed out, (I'm not sure which). I woke to a German shep-herd's teeth in my skin and ten angry cops with guns drawn, daring me to move. Their commands of, "Don't move!" must've been the dog's green light to find a new spot to munch on, because he nearly ate poor ole Dano before it was over. Back in those days, running from the cops was a misdemeanor, so because I had no dope on me, I bonded out and returned home to heal.

One morning before one of many court dates, my lawyer called to tell me there was a federal warrant out for my arrest. When you receive something that reads, 'The United States of America vs. your sorry hide', it's unsettling to say the least. Apparently, I had hacked off the entire United States. Normal folks would be scared to death by this, and I must admit I was a little worried. But in my dope-fogged mind, I figured all I needed was lots of money to buy my way out (as if I could). So, I set out to make a barrel of money before they caught me. Two years later when they *did* come for me, I had money and a whole lot of dope in me. I was tired and had lost everything I ever loved. To top things off, I had become someone I would've hated in my early days. Yet there I was. It was almost a relief that it was coming to an end.

I still didn't make it easy for them. Despite threats of twenty-five to life and the games they played to get me to talk, I kept my mouth shut (because all roads led back to me). Back in those days, a snitch was the lowest form of life there was. I wasn't about to tell on anyone—especially myself. As it turned out, they didn't have a whole lot on me so they gave me a few years to sit and think about my life choices. Up to this point, my longest stay in county jails across mid–to–northern Missouri was a few days, weeks, or a month or two. This country boy had much to learn in a real short time. I was now in with the big boys. Luckily, my bunkie was an old, seasoned convict (an OG) who gladly showed me the ropes.

When I got out, I felt pretty confident I would never return to my previous lifestyle. And I didn't for almost four years. Until someone asked me at a birthday party if I wanted to do a line. I was just drunk enough to think, *surely once couldn't hurt.* So, I did. Boom! Next day, I bought an eight ball and was back in the game. Stupid hurts. It wasn't long before the cops targeted me, and once again I had thrown a whole new life away.

I preferred traveling gravel roads because I could drive a hundred miles per hour and the dust kicked up behind me was good cover. If I couldn't outdrive the cops (which most times I did), I'd take off on foot. They, being a little on the plump side, usually didn't last long.

Except for one state trooper in particular. I just couldn't shake him. He tried the old pit maneuver on me and somehow missed. That put him in front of me. I returned the favor by putting him in the ditch. My joy was short-lived because when I topped the hill afterward, there were more. To make matters worse, he had recovered and was now behind me. That's when I learned that highway patrolmen aren't your average donut-eating law enforcement officers. They chased me through woods, across creeks, through thorns; I couldn't get more than a couple-hundred feet ahead of them. Finally, having run out of steam, I laid on my stomach with my arms spread and braced for impact. No bracing could've prepared me for what came next. Not only did they crack my ribs, but the six-foot-six, two-hundred-seventy-five pound one I'd tangled with came crashing in with his knee to my jaw. They put me in an ambulance and took me to the hospital.

Later, on my way to jail, I told 'Sasquatch' that if they would lower my charge to a misdemeanor, I'd claim that my injuries happened when I ran into a tree while running from them. One month later, I was released with timed served . . . only to turn around and spend thirteen months in a four-man cell of yet another county jail, looking up at, "Kill Yourself" scratched into the underside of the bunk above me. I removed it before I left.

Despite my resolve to never return, I was in the middle of nowhere, with no place to live, and no transportation. My PO expected me to report twice a month and land a job within thirty days. Or go back to jail. So, I cleaned afterbirth and hog manure out of pens at a hog farm for $8.00 an hour. Every day, I walked the eight miles to work and back from the abandoned building where I stayed. Twice a month, I hitched a ride to my PO thirty miles away (all the while, knowing I could make some real money the old way). But I held on tight. With my first paycheck, I purchased a ten-speed bike (at a garage sale), and some decent food for a change. The rest, I saved. My next check two weeks later covered a $300 piece-of-junk truck and the $200 deposit on a rat-infested apartment.

Living was tight, but things were looking up. I had received a raise and wasn't high or in jail . . . so there was that. But thoughts of how far I'd come from having a farm and family nagged at me; they would've destroyed me had I allowed myself to go there. Neither could I shake the constant emptiness I felt inside. Having grown up in a Christian home, I knew about the Lord. I'd seen Him in action through my parents' continuous love and prayers for me.

I turned to whiskey to keep those thoughts at bay. But that didn't always work. When I started hanging out with younger women who liked to get drunk and high, I knew it was just a matter of time before it came for me too. I needed to get out of there. My mother's prayers were constantly battling with my dope demons, and no matter how much whiskey I drank I couldn't outrun any of them.

I transferred my probation to Jackson County Missouri and landed a job there installing windows at $15.00 an hour. My drinking also slowed. That's when I met the cutest and most remarkable woman. Not only was Melanie a blast to be with, but she matched me in every way, from drinking as much as me, to riding a Harley as well as anyone. I fell head-over-heels in love. She even had a praying grandmother! So, we drank. That is, until she started going to church. Her drinking also slowed. A month or so later, she came home from church and looked me dead in the eye and said, "I can't be with a man who won't go to church with me."

Wait! What? The next Sunday came around and she announced, "We're going to church." I was scared, not of actually going, but of all the thoughts and silent prayers I had carried with me over the years. Had I waited too long? gone too far? After the awful things I'd done, surely God wouldn't let me just walk in and pretend all was well. I was afraid to let myself feel His presence. What if I started crying and wasn't able to stop? But the Holy Spirit wouldn't stop tugging at my heart. So I went, fighting back the tears. When it was over, I was happy to have survived. After a few months of going, I noticed my drinking had all but stopped. And we were actually happy.

One day after church, I got alone and invited Jesus back into my life. I wept and repented for all the things I'd done. I promised I would serve Him if He would guide me and use me for His glory. I thanked Him for being there and keeping me safe all those years. I thanked Him for hearing an old woman's prayers for her son, and an old woman's prayers for her granddaughter. I thanked Him for placing Melanie in my path.

Although Melanie was out on pretrial release because of her own past, I couldn't help but fall in love with her. In spite of everything going on, we decided to get married. With her about to begin her eight-year course in decision making with the federal government (we call it "College"), and with both of us starting a life serving the Lord, we knew things would be difficult—and by worldly standards, almost impossible. She told me that the only way we would make it through this time apart, was to surrender our hearts and lives to the Lord. She was one-hundred-percent correct. So, we decided to talk with someone who could relate. That's when the Lord led us to Ray and Lisa Stribling, pastors of Hope City KC. They gave us good, sound advice and prayed with us. Since then, we've become not only family, but very dear friends. I also met an old gangster at Hope City. I have much respect for Bill Corum and have come to love him and seek his council. I appreciate the Lord making our paths cross.

Hebrews 11:1 *Faith is being sure of what we hope for and certain of things we do not see.* At the time of this writing, Melanie is entering the fourth year of her eight-year bit in BOP. And every day I think, *today might be the day God brings her home.* Our waiting on the Lord has made her one of the strongest women of faith I've ever known. Her faith gives me faith to carry on day after day. She says the same of me.

But there *are* times when she gets discouraged and wonders if she's really making a difference in prison. Is God really using her to minister to others? Does He hear her prayers for them? I understand her feelings of hopelessness and frustration because of my history of being locked up. But God loves us. He *does* hear our prayers for others and *does* use the smallest of things we do and say to glorify His name. We tend to think we must say great prayers and do mighty things to be heard, but in reality, it's usually the small, humble things that have the greatest impact.

God confirmed that not long ago when I received a Christmas card from a girl named Sophia. She said that seven days after my wife was transferred to another prison, Covid 19 struck. Every girl in Melanie's former housing unit became sick. Some were very ill—including Sophia. One day while Sophia was praying for her friend Melanie and praying Melanie would still remember them all in her prayers like she did every night before they moved her, she noticed a note on her locker. She got up to check it out. It said, "Abandon hope for faith," Love Mel. Sophia immediately began to cry. The other girls cried when she showed it to them. From that point on, they began feeling better. In a few short days, all were back on their feet with no symptoms. When I delivered Sophia's message of thanks to my wife, she lost it. Not only did God protect her from Covid, but He heard her prayers for her friends. That's just one story of God's faithfulness to us.

Another time, while on my way home from visiting Melanie, I stopped for gas in a small town. A car pulled up opposite me at the pump, and a small, elderly gentleman got out. He looked as though he might fall over dead at any moment. Yet, he had a gentle smile. When I noticed him looking at my license plate—me, who knows no stranger, asked him how he was doing. Ignoring my question, he asked what part of Missouri I was from. I told him Kansas City. It turned out he was also headed there to locate his children and other family members he hadn't seen in years. Because of excessive drinking, Cirrhosis in his liver had turned to cancer. With only three to six weeks left to live he was on an urgent mission to set things right with his family.

Choking back tears, I thought, *I need to tell this man about a loving Savior and a merciful Father*! But before I could say anything, he said, "I know it ain't none of my business, but time being short, I just gotta ask . . . do you know the Lord? And if not, would you like to meet Him?" I had to laugh because now I knew *why* he had that warm smile. I told him that I *did* know the Lord, and that I was about to ask him the same thing. He had given his heart to the Lord before he learned of his cancer. Now, he needed to reconcile with the family he abandoned years ago. His hopes were that they would forgive. More importantly, he wanted them saved and would I agree with him in prayer concerning this? He said he read somewhere in the Bible that if two or more agree together, it would be done (Mathew 18:19). He prayed a very simple but beautiful prayer, and I agreed with him (Amen!). We parted with him saying, "Thank you, son. I'll see you in glory!"

"Yes sir, you will!" I answered.

As we get older, we worry about our children. Did we give them what it takes to make it? I spent thirty-plus years running from God. Made a mess out of my life and my family's. But just a couple of years after surrendering my life to the Lord, all my children were speaking to me. All are now clean and sober. It's not too late for you.

Not long ago, I got my old street glide out and took a trip. Work was a little slow and my birthday was approaching. Why not? I packed light, not intending to go far or be gone long. The weather looked good north of Kansas City. So, north I went. Well, one place led to another, and another until I found myself in the Black Hills of South Dakota. I'd gone this far, why stop now? The speed limit was eighty mph, so I set my cruise on eighty three and headed for Wyoming.

When I blew past a sheriff sitting at a stop sign and gave him the how-you-doing nod, he hit his lights and followed. Although it's been ten-plus years since I had any trouble with cops, it still freaks me out when they're behind me. To complicate matters, I (for whatever reason) never got my motorcycle license. This big, older cop with cowboy hat and an actual six gun on his hip pulled me over and informed me that the speed limit on that stretch of highway was sixty mph. While he ran my license, I figured, *well . . . this is going to be expensive. I'll be lucky to ride away.* When he handed it back, saying, "Well, you're not wanted", I was relieved to say the least. He then asked about the shirt I was wearing. I told him it was a prison-ministry shirt, and that sometimes I go with my friend Bill Corum into prisons to share Christ with our brothers and sisters. As it turned out, the sheriff and some of his buddies did the same in his state. He had me follow him back to town and he bought my lunch. Not only did we have a good talk, but I made a new friend. No ticket either. Didn't see that coming!

The family of God is huge. The blessings of being under His protection are huge as well. What I'm saying is, when you surrender your life to Christ you enter into His blessings and protection. And into His family.

I've been clean from dope for thirteen years and from alcohol for five. God has given me a wonderful wife who is serving Him from prison. He has restored our relationship with our children and has blessed us with grandchildren. You may think it's impossible to ever experience love, peace, joy, and family because of what you've done. But take it from an old ex-con who thought he'd gone too far from God's reach—everything is possible if you come to Him on His terms and with humility. He loves me. He loves you too.

Are you ready to begin a new life? That feeling you are experiencing right now is the Holy Spirit inviting you. Please don't turn Him away. Your life and your family depend on it. I pray you will invite Him in. You will be amazed at how much He loves you. My prayers and love go out to each and every one of you.

Contact:

Dan Brisbin

c/o Prison Power Ministries

PO Box 281

Lone Jack, MO 64070

RUDE BOY

BREWEL CURRIE

MY MOTHER RAISED ME in 'the ways of the Lord'. My father taught me work ethic. When I left home at the age of eighteen, I chose neither. I decided to live a life of sin and death. I used my God-given gifts for evil and became a drug dealer, a drug addict, an alcoholic, and ended up trapped in the circumstances that sin had created in my life. My behavior caused not only destruction in my own life but in the lives of others. This lifestyle resulted in me serving altogether thirteen-plus years in prison.

As a young boy, I had a vision of myself living in prison. I even told my mother about it. Decades later, when the door to my maximum-security cell at Lansing Correctional Facility opened, it came back to me. This cell I was entering was the exact one in my childhood vision. I believe God gave me that vision so I could later share with the world that even through the worst of times, if we surrender our lives to Him, the good things He planned from the beginning are still there waiting for us.

My life of drugs and sin kept me going in and out of jail and prison. Despite the many opportunities given me to change my ways, I never accepted them. After my second time in the Kansas prisons, I was allowed an interstate compact release to Virginia, where my biological father lived. There, I wasn't required to report to a parole officer, but was to call in. Because I didn't even do that, I had an outstanding warrant and was on the run again. In order to keep out of the public eye, I never used my real name—on jobs or with the women I was seeing.

Eventually, I caught a new case in Virginia. I finished that sentence in a county jail without even going to prison there. US Marshalls then came to extradite me back to Kansas. Kansas—again—gave me another chance. The judge knew my parents and told me that if I lived with them, he would place me on probation. Once again, I didn't follow through and was sentenced to sixty months.

I only had to serve two years. Afterward, I decided to give up selling drugs. When my youngest daughter was an infant, I had another vision. In this one, I was being arrested with my baby girl in my arms. When I told my wife about it, she thought it was crazy because I wasn't selling drugs anymore. But I was using them. Someone tipped my parole officer off and he ordered a house search. The police came while I was feeding my one-month-old daughter her bottle. Just like in the vision, she was in my arms. They found my marijuana hidden beneath her crib. Because I was once again being arrested, I had to call my wife so she could come home to be with our daughter. This was the lowest point in my life.

I called on the name of Jesus. Because I finally surrendered to His way of life, He changed me. By His mercy, I am free from sin and death. I have hope and a future that I know only He can give.

It was during my last incarceration that I received my calling to be a minister. My ministry actually began at the local parole office while I was a parolee and has carried on through today. I am a street prophet—called to be a light through my words and deeds wherever I go. I am to preach God's life-changing Word and tell everyone about His saving grace.

God has redeemed in my life in so many wonderful ways:

1. God redeemed me physically—This was after having gone to jail and prison over and over again, never being able to stay out for any length of time. After having served a five-year sentence, followed by another three-year sentence with only one year free in between.

2. God redeemed me financially—Because I worked on and off between prison sentences, I did not file taxes for seven years. Upon release (as a Christian), I found a tax professional and was honest with him. I explained that I had just been released from prison and my credit was a mess. He filed all seven years for me. Because of God's favor, he let me pay him whatever I could each month. Within five-years' time, my credit was miraculously redeemed. I now own a big home in a new housing development.

3. God redeemed my career path—Due to my previous felonies, I could only get jobs working in restaurants. Through Christ's miracles, the state hired me as a mentor to troubled teens at a boys' group home. That made me the state's employee while technically still a parolee under their supervision. God then moved me to a higher government position as a supervisor at Job Corps, where I educate, mentor, and assist in changing the lives of young people ages sixteen to twenty-four. Because I was faithful, God promoted me to Job Corps Residential Living Manager, overseeing three departments. I equip our students to grow socially and spiritually, to become everything God created them to be—to become great!

Because of my previous life of sin, I was two classes short of earning my bachelor's degree in college. God, through Christ, redeemed my education. While seeking a way to complete my degree, I received a phone call from the school advisor. He informed me that the college would give me my bachelor's degree, eliminating the need to finish those two classes. It was a miracle. I am now pursuing my master's degree in Business Administration.

4. God redeemed my broken relationships—Before surrendering to Christ, my relationships with my parents, my wife, and children, were dead. Christ restored all of them by making me into the man He called me to be—a man of love, understanding, and prayer. My relationship with my father was restored just months before he passed. My mother told me I would be the one who would lead him to Christ. And she was right. Hallelujah! As a child and young adult, I had harbored anger and mistrust toward him. But the man I once hated and thought wanted nothing good for me, became my biggest cheerleader. He was the one God used to open the door for my job at Job Corps. I have the peace of knowing he was a believer when he passed.

My relationship with my oldest daughter has been restored as well. Because she had seen me leave twice to go to prison, I needed to gain her trust again. Christ taught me how to be gentle and kind, how to respond in love to her mistrust. Through Him, I was able to show her what a true father looks like and she accepted me. Our relationship was restored.

My infant daughter was four when I returned home from prison for the last time. I hadn't seen her at all during my last incarceration. With Christ's help, I learned to become her father in person.

Letters from my wife were few while I was in prison because she was taking care of our baby and working on her own. But she saw the change in me before I returned home. Previously, I had been spoiled in prison with phone calls, letters, visits, and money always coming in. During my last incarceration, I refused to spend my family's money.

I was able to go to work release and sent money home instead. I was proud to be a true man of God and put my family first. God, in turn, faithfully provided for my own needs through indigent packages. He taught me how to let go of earthly possessions and rely on Him for everything. He revealed to me my purpose and taught me how to be a father and a husband.

5. God redeemed my soul—Before Christ, I didn't know who I was. All the years in and out of incarceration and living a lifestyle of sin, I couldn't escape the feeling that *This isn't me. I'm just playing a part.* Because of my childhood visions, I was scared of my potential, scared of who I really was. I tried being everything the world said I should be, but it was all a lie. Because our lives are given to us through Christ—and only through Christ—nothing else will work. In Christ, I now see what is true and what is a lie. I no longer stand on what the world says, but on what God says about me. Rude Boy (tough guy, rebel, gangsta, criminal), no longer describes me.

I know who I am and Whose I am. I'm a child of God, a man with a great purpose. Almighty God gave me that purpose and no one can take it away. My mind is strong in Christ. My emotions don't make my decisions; my will is surrendered to Him.

Graduating with my bachelor's degree, being ordained as a minister, and buying a new house all happened the fifth year of my release from prison. Five is the number of favor—God's favor. They were all part of God's plan for my life.

We are created for God's glory. Everything we say and do should be to glorify His name. He is worthy of all our praise! God saved me to serve Him and to be a light to the world. I seek, through my ministry, to reveal Jesus and make an impact that changes lives for the better. For we are God's masterpiece. He has created us anew in Christ Jesus so we can do the good things He planned for us long ago. *For we are God's handiwork, created in Christ Jesus to do good works, which God prepared in advance for us to do* (Ephesians 2:10).

Contact Information:
Brewel Currie
PO Box 482
Junction City, KS 66441

ASH PITS AND ALLEY APPLES

MIKE BROGAN

I WAS BORN AND RAISED IN ST. LOUIS, MISSOURI. Some of my earliest memories center around living on the eleventh floor of one of the high-rise buildings in the now infamous Pruitt-Igoe housing projects. It was in the mid-1950s and I was between seven and nine years old. Since we lived at the far end of the top floor, I had to make my way through the building, and through the entire project grounds to reach the city streets leading to my school. There were no school buses in those days, so I was forced to walk the ten blocks through some of the city's roughest neighborhoods in order get to school.

There were fights to and from school and fights on the playgrounds that first year we lived there. I took many alternate routes in order to avoid them and could have drawn a detailed map of the gangways, alleyways, back yards, and city streets in that whole neighborhood. However, it soon became obvious that my only real choice was to fight as hard as I could or get beat up regularly. Bullies tended to run in packs, so running or trying to hide didn't do much good.

As I learned to fight back—out of sheer necessity—I also began to develop a bad attitude and an anger problem. Although I had two older cousins, I was the oldest of a new generation of Brogans in our family. For all intents and purposes, most of my role models were adults with plenty of lifestyle-behavior problems of their own. After what I'd observed of them, I began to believe that hanging out in beer joints, getting drunk, and cheating on your spouse was normal behavior.

When I was ten years old, we moved out of the high-rise projects and into a little house on Obear Street in North St. Louis, just a few blocks west of the Mississippi River and North Broadway. Back then, we seldom lived anywhere for more than a year or two, so making lasting friendships was difficult. Each new location had its own set of problems, and this place was no exception.

To-and-from-school fights were frequent, an unavoidable way of life in our new neighborhood. Soon after we moved in, I discovered that the neighborhood bully just so happened to live in the house next door. At age thirteen, Gary was already over six-feet tall—a good head-and-shoulders taller than me, and three years older. His favorite pastime was to show every new kid in the neighborhood just how tough he was for his age. His parents didn't seem to care how many fights he started, as long as their son didn't come out on the losing end.

My cousin, Chuck, lived a short distance from us on Florissant Ave. He was three years older than me, and thankfully was eager to teach his little cousin how best to defend himself against bullies. Since I was rapidly accumulating way more than my fair share of fat lips and black eyes, I was just as eager to learn how to put an end to my dilemma. Chuck's father had been a boxer, so Chuck's training in boxing began when he was old enough to make a fist. He fought well. After giving me a few lessons, I figured I was ready to teach that bully neighbor a lesson the next time he decided to fatten my lips and black my eyes. It didn't work out quite the way I planned it. Because I intended to show him how skilled I'd become at boxing, he proceeded to beat me up even worse.

I had just about had enough of getting beat up by this clown! The next boxing lesson Chuck gave me also came with some practical advice on how to teach someone bigger than myself a lesson once and for all. St. Louis was famous for having a lot of "ash pits" in the alleyways behind houses in residential neighborhoods. Most of these old ash pits were made of bricks that had fallen out of the walls. These bricks (commonly called "alley apples"), littered the alley much like apples fallen from trees. The next time Gary tried to use me as his punching bag, I was ready for him. I picked up a couple alley apples and told him he would be eating them without any teeth if he ever hit me again. That incident marked the end of my problem with bullies. But my own anger problem and criminal activities were just beginning.

The rest of my childhood and young adulthood was virtually filled with drugs, alcohol, theft, burglaries, armed robberies, sex, and violence. I became so uncontrollable that I spent more time in jail than out. They sent me to reform school three different times before I reached my sixteenth birthday. After being released from my third trip, I got married and started a family at the tender age of seventeen.

My father and mother were geographically separated when I got out of reform school. Dad had moved to the Loop area in Chicago, where he landed a good job with Inter-Ocean Terminals on State Street across from one of the main police precincts. I remember the police station in particular. On its roof was a giant blue light that revolved just like the ones on top of Chicago's patrol cars. My mother had moved back into the housing projects with my three younger sisters and three younger brothers. These projects were more like apartment houses and duplexes rather than the high-rise projects we lived in when I was younger.

The lifestyle I chose, along with the problems that inevitably follow those kinds of choices, had not yet reached their climax. For the next few years, I continued violating both man's and God's laws with little-to-no regard for the consequences of my actions. Adding to my previously mentioned crimes and immoral activities, I became a bodyguard for one of the largest drug dealers in the greater St. Louis area. Aside from being extremely dangerous, this activity made it easier and more convenient for me to increase my own drug usage. Putting a needle in my arm, along with my intense criminal activities, soon landed me in one of America's historically bloodiest prisons for five more years of my still very young life.

Up until that first trip to prison in 1967 when I was twenty years old, I was somewhat oblivious to the fact that I had been on one, long fast track to self-destruction. With a clear mind, and lots of time to think about the wrong choices I'd made up until that pivotal point, I decided to choose a more positive and productive lifestyle for the future. The Missouri Department of Corrections, in cooperation with several colleges and universities who taught courses at the prison, were generous enough to provide me with all the schooling I could ever soak up in those five years.

Day after day, I sat in my cell contemplating and planning a better life for my remaining years on earth. Yet, I had no idea—nor could I have ever guessed—what God had planned for me. I think I always believed there was a God, but I had never fully examined the likelihood of living my life in compliance with His supreme will for me. In fact, had I known what would happen to turn my life upside down in the next few years, I might have disagreed with His plans. Isaiah 55:8–9 says, *"For My thoughts are not your thoughts, and your ways are not My ways," says the Lord. "For as the heavens are higher than the earth, so are My ways higher than your ways, and My thoughts than your thoughts.".*

His thoughts, plans, and ways are always infinitely better than anything any of us could ever devise without Him to guide us. Unless we are completely sold out to His will, we will seldom agree with a God who knows everything past, present, and future. I had devised what I believed was a great plan of action. So, I diligently studied a variety of academic courses, joined the prison boxing team, lifted weights, exercised, and ran five-to-ten miles nearly every day of the week. There were also a few valuable building trades I picked up that have proved a great blessing to me through the years.

I think the most heartbreaking news of my life was when I was told that my wife, the mother of my three children, had been intentionally killed by a drug dealer in St. Louis. Before going to prison, I had spent a couple of years protecting this same type of person who murdered her. In a very revealing and strange sort of way, God conveyed a message that reached deep into my heart and made me understand just how serious and destructive the consequences of sin really are. He showed me how the toppling dominoes of a sinful life can, and often do, cause a great deal more harm than we see when we disobey our Creator.

I will always be grateful to God, in this life and the next, that He did not allow me to blame Him for this tragedy. Instead, He continued to speak to my innermost being, making me realize that there was a purpose in what happened, and that I would see it better as the future unfolded. With an abundance of tears and a broken heart, I asked God to open the right doors for me to do His will. I promised to do my best to walk through them and follow His wisdom and guidance for my life.

In the years and decades following that simple prayer, God continued to open door after door for me to follow Him. While still doing time in prison, He opened a door for me to work in a juvenile-justice program that had been developed by an outside prison ministry. I was also invited to speak to several groups of teachers and students in small-town schools in Southern Missouri. When I got out, He gave me the opportunity to be a youth counselor for the juvenile court system. The most important door of all was when He led some precious saints to do an outreach to the kids in the detention center where I worked. Because of their obedience to *go and preach the gospel to every creature* (Mark16:15), I attended their church revival meeting that night in Raytown, Missouri and gave my heart to Jesus. He then opened the door for me to enter Christian ministry and share Jesus with precious folks in my family, in prisons, churches, juvenile institutions, and many other places.

At the time of this writing, I am seventy-three-years young. I have a wonderful wife, an abundant blessing of children, grandchildren, great-grandchildren, and many other family members. My greatest desire is to see all of them in heaven someday. I fully intend to keep preaching *Christ and Him crucified for our salvation*, until I walk through those gates of Heaven that Jesus opened for all who trust Him as Lord and Savior.

You can read Mike's whole story in his book: *Pulling No Punches*.

Contact Information:
Mike Brogan
c/o Prison Power Ministries
PO Box 281
Lone Jack, MO 64070

HOPE'S UP

SHANNON WEST

How did I end up here? Where did everything go wrong? How could I have been so lost in life? I was AWOL from the military, in a state far from home, hanging around people who only cared about where to get their next fix, and now I was on the verge of dying because someone shot me with a .38 pistol from seven feet away.

BEFORE

Looking back over my life, I knew I was not supposed to be in this kind of mess when nothing terribly traumatic had happened that would cause me to make such poor choices. Even though my parents divorced when I was ten years old, I wasn't raised in a bad home. My mother loved me very much and I remember being raised fairly strict by her. My passion was playing soccer with my neighborhood friends. So, every night after school we met for a soccer game on the street in front of our houses. It was a great childhood.

The day I reached the age of accountability, I was with my step-brother (from my father's second marriage), and a group of his friends. We saw a bike at a bowling alley. Since it wasn't locked up, they decided it would be fun to take it. Because I was the youngest, and more than likely wanted to impress the older boys, they chose me to ride the bike to a place where we could hide it. I had never done anything like this before. Though in my gut I knew this was wrong, the excitement I felt was overwhelming. So, I went along without a second thought. Little did I know that at that moment, that impulsive decision opened me up to a life of bondage to the enemy. From that time on, he worked overtime to keep me on a path I was not created to travel.

Although it would be years before that seed began to sprout . . . sprout it did! For fifteen years, I was stuck in a cocaine addiction that completely destroyed my life. I did things I knew were wrong and downright evil, but it did not change the way I lived. I ended up losing everything and everyone I had ever cared for. I was divorced, had failed to be the father I should be to my daughter, and my mother was at her wits' end with me. My life was swirling downward to an unimaginable place of despair. I cannot tell you how many times I thought about just ending it all. The only problem was that my father had committed suicide and I remembered how disgusted I was with him for ending his life like that. Yet, there I was thinking the same thought?

Somehow, I escaped those temptations to self-destruct; I never followed through with purposely trying to end my life. But I continued putting enormous amounts of mind-altering substances into my body, attempting to fill the emptiness I'd felt for so much of my life.

Finally, one day I asked myself the question, "How did I get here?". I was tired of getting high, tired of aimlessly running the streets, tired of hanging with people who would do anything to anyone just to get high, tired of not being able to escape. I was tired! tired! tired! Later that afternoon, while standing in the kitchen at the house where I was staying, staring into the dining room at the people sitting around the table, I thought, *I don't like any of those people and they do not like me. The only reason we are all together is because of the drugs on that table.* And at that very moment I looked up and said, "If you are real, get me out of this life!"

It was the first time I actually searched for a God I knew nothing about. I believed He existed—vaguely—and that was because I knew evil existed. If there was evil, surely there had to be good. Right? That was the extent of it. Nothing extravagant, no lengthy prayer or anything. Just a simple statement. Then, I went back to doing what I had always done—getting high.

Well, that prayer was answered just a few, short months later when the judge gave me a fifty-five-month prison sentence. I was now faced with the choice to get to know the One I had prayed to or be mad at how my prayer was answered.

I chose to get to know Him. So, that is exactly what I did. I sent a request to the chaplain for a Bible. When I received it, the first thing I noticed was the cover. The picture on front was of two hands in a set of handcuffs with the chain broken. Beneath were the words, *Free On the Inside*. I thought to myself, *I have never even been free on the outside*! I began reading that Bible daily, and one day fell to my knees and cried to God to forgive me. Right there inside that cell, God Himself introduced me to His Son, Jesus. I accepted Him as my Lord, and I have never looked back.

AFTER

When I got out of prison, I returned to my hometown of Wichita, KS. I must admit to feeling a little nervous. Not scared, but nervous. I knew I was a completely different person. I no longer had the desires that once drove me to do those things that almost destroyed me and everything around me. But living this new life outside the walls was uncharted territory. I felt like a fish out of water.

I am so thankful that God had already placed a woman in my life for me to lean on and grow with. Years prior to getting out, LaDonna and I wrote letters to each other. We started off friends and fell in love. Little did I know the big role she would play when life on the outside began moving too fast. Just a little over a year after being released, I relapsed. All I can say is that one, seemingly small wrong choice led to a full-blown three-month relapse. I was *again*, losing everything God had placed in my life. One day I finally asked myself, *what are you doing*? I had reverted back to the world I'd known so well, and the demons were having their way with me. Despite my shame over getting high the night before, I managed to get up the courage to call LaDonna and ask her to come over and pray for me.

And she came—not knowing exactly what she would encounter when she arrived. She ended up staying the night with me, praying. I slept like a baby. Of course, she has a different account of what happened. Like a straight soldier, she stayed the course, doing nothing but holding onto me, and praying throughout the night.

When I woke up the next morning, we packed some of my belongings and headed to Valley Hope Treatment Center. I felt like a complete loser. I had come so far and had learned so much . . . how could I have let this happen? They assigned me a temporary room until I caught up on my sleep. When I moved into my permanent room, something happened that changed the course of my life again—this time, forever.

As I walked into that permanent room, I noticed a Bible setting on the nightstand and instantly felt like Jesus said to my heart, "How did you expect to win the war without your sword, son?" That's when it hit me. I had read the Word of God every day during my incarceration; I was full of the knowledge it taught me. However, I hadn't picked the Bible up one time since my release. The knowledge was in my head, but because I stopped feeding my spirit, the enemy had waited till I grew weak so he could pounce on me.

Since then, I have never stopped being in the Word of God. And have *never* had the urge to use drugs again. I was instantly set free from the bondage of addiction. The remainder of my time at the treatment center was spent with a smile on my face and in my heart while I witnessed to many people. In fact, the good path I am on came full circle. One year after graduating from Valley Hope, I returned to celebrate my first year clean and sober. I have since then had the honor of going back and visiting a couple of times and sharing about the awesome miracle I experienced while there.

It took a few years for me to feel comfortable sharing my journey with others. I worked at a car dealership, where at times it wasn't so easy to live for Christ. However, with me making right choices in those every-day decisions we must all make, life became manageable. Jesus carried me through the tough times.

In 2012, LaDonna and I decided to go together on a mission trip with an incredible organization called Global Ventures. Having never done anything like that, I wasn't even sure I would be approved for a passport. But when God has a mission for you—He moves mountains. We spent eleven days in a little city about an hour and a half outside of Bangkok, ministering in schools and marketplaces. Each evening, we took part in amazing crusade events.

What we witnessed during that trip changed my walk with Christ forever. I saw physical miracles that could never happen—but God. Hundreds heard about Jesus Christ for the first time and accepted Him as their Lord and Savior. Interestingly enough, God used that trip to Bangkok to set me on my destiny path. When the leaders of Global Ventures heard about my story, they arranged for me to go into a Thai prison and speak to a group of prisoners. There I was, in another country, not only representing Jesus but sharing my testimony in a prison! I did the best I could, and despite having to use a translator, seven men accepted Jesus Christ into their hearts. That's when I *knew* that all of my terrible, destitute, destructive years could actually be used for good when they're used for the Kingdom of God.

I've visited many United States prisons since 2012. And we've seen God do miracle after miracle, not only in my own life but in countless others. My wife and I have held weekly services in the women's prison in Topeka KS for years. God is using us to show his beautiful creation of women that Kingdom men are real. He is using my life to give them hope.

At the time of this writing, I am celebrating my twelfth complete year of sobriety, and have helped lead thousands to make the decision to accept Jesus Christ as Lord. I am thankful every day for the saving grace Jesus gave me. I pass on to you the life standard I strive to live by each-and-every day: If He woke me up again today, then He is not done with me yet. So, today I will represent Him well, and be ready to share the saving grace of Jesus Christ with everyone He brings across my path.

I pray that my story helps you find the same freedom I've found in Jesus.

Contact Information:
Shannon West
3811 N Meridian
Wichita KS 67204

CRAZY CABLE MAN

JOHNNY ALLEN

I WAS BORN IN 1957, the middle child of a dysfunctional family. My siblings and I were the poor kids on the block. Our alcoholic dad abused us verbally, physically, and mentally. Our mother, despite her codependency on him, loved us and did her best to keep us safe, fed, and comfortable. That was everyday life in our household.

That is, until the day my dad embarrassed and humiliated me in front of my whole school. I was twelve years old when that happened. Looking back on it, I place no blame on him, but from then on, I made all my own decisions. Later that same evening (after dad passed out and mom was taking care of him), I snuck out with some older neighborhood kids and smoked pot. I also took my first drink, and loved how it made all the hurt, pain, and shame disappear. From that night on, drinking became my new coping mechanism that carried me through the next thirty-eight years. If I didn't like the way I felt (which turned out to be most of the time), I changed how I felt by altering my mind.

This seemed to work well through my high-school years, but I also picked up other habits like lying, stealing, and manipulating. If I wanted something, I took it. During that time, I was also introduced to and fell in love with cocaine, heroin, hashish, crystal meth, LSD, masculine, PCP, and acid. Because I was still able to function, I didn't realize I had become a drug addict.

Right out of high school, I got married. The girl was sixteen; I was twenty. Because she was pregnant, my choices were marriage or jail. After the birth of our son, I introduced her to my world of drugs. Now, not only did I have a sex partner, but a using partner—and a convenient caregiver for my son so I could continue in my ways that had now turned criminal.

Affairs, dealing, robbing, stealing, burglaries, and late-night escapades were all kept hidden, using my job with the local cable television company as coverup. I made use of company vehicles to transport drugs, my office to distribute, and the warehouse to hide contents and proceeds. As far as anyone knew, I was living a normal life.

In 1983, our twin daughters were born very premature, and required extended hospitalization. I continued living my double lifestyle. Because I stayed gone much of the time, my wife turned back to the drugs she'd stopped taking during her pregnancy and became highly addicted to crystal meth over the next two years. She eventually grew violent, depressed, antisocial, and bipolar, which led to her being institutionalized several times and unable to face reality. I—their drug-intoxicated father—was left to care for our three young children. This arrangement had failure written all over it. And fail, I did. Thankfully, my mom took care of them while I worked, partied, and lived in my corrupt little world.

I hid behind the mask of Little League coach, soccer coach, and helping in other youth sports, (still believing I was fooling people into thinking I was a normal person). I joined the Elks Club, was a noonday Optimist, a master manipulator, and con artist . . . or so I thought.

In late 1992, I started freebasing cocaine. Not long after, I was on the needle. I learned to cook crack cocaine and discovered its power over people, especially women. Profits from distribution were also addicting. I became a full-blown junkie. With my two best friends (the needle and the pipe), I crossed the line from sanity to insanity. I had no conscience—didn't care who I hurt, stole from, or robbed. Like a tornado on steroids, I was self-destructing fast.

In 1993, I was caught embezzling around $30,000 from my employer. I made a feeble attempt at recovery, hoping they'd take pity on a poor drug addict who had lost his way. They didn't. I ended up back in prison for the fourth time since 1986.

The year 1993 was the beginning of the end for ole Johnny Allen. From 1993–2003 my life consisted of divorce, loss of family, jobs, homes, automobiles, and finances. County jail became my short-term home thirty-some times, prison stays five times. My heart was sick, and chicken-noodle soup wasn't going to cure it.

On January 3, 2003, in a back room at my mom and dad's house, I was awakened to a Pettis County Sheriff deputy standing over me with a pistol in my face. He arrested me for first-degree armed robbery. This began the most incredible journey of my life. Let me explain.

As we pulled into the old Missouri State Penitentiary for the fifth time, a transporting officer who knew me by name (if they know you by name, you've been doing bad too long) said to me, "Allen, read it one more time." The sign read: You Are Now Entering the Missouri State Prison—Leave All Your Hopes and Dreams Behind. I chuckled because, of course, I had no hopes. No dreams. For the next year and some months, I lived life as I had on the streets—conning and manipulating in order to stay high and keep hopeless feelings from surfacing.

Here is where I start getting excited. You see, if you're reading this, you have probably lived parts of my old life and there's nothing about that life that would encourage you. It was full of brokenness and hopelessness. So, I will stop here with all that, and begin with that incredible journey I spoke of a few minutes ago.

The middle of 2004, the Missouri State Penitentiary closed. We were moved to the new Jefferson City Correctional Center. With this move came a loss of what little freedom we had. At the old place, we were allowed quite a bit of time to ourselves. Activities were plentiful—legal and illegal. The new prison, on the other hand, was twenty-two-hours-a-day lockdown at the beginning, with ten-minute phone calls and ten-minute showers. Trips to and from the chow hall three times a day, and fake medical visits were my only other shots at getting a break from my cell. It *did* get better later on when other activities were added, but I wasn't used to this way of jailing.

When I started looking for other outlets, I found out that if you got a job, you could move around the institution a few hours a day. I also learned that those jobs were scarce. Most had long waiting lists because in a max prison no one leaves. But the con man in me convinced a maintenance man that I was skilled enough that if one day the prison were to fall down, I could rebuild it. Thankfully, I didn't have to prove myself, because I didn't know the hot water valve from the cold. But God was positioning me for my miracle.

It was through that job that I met the chaplain of the prison. One Sunday on my way to medical, I walked by the chapel and heard music coming out of a door that wasn't supposed to be open. Talk about God's perfect timing. When I saw the chaplain the next time, I asked him what the music and everything was about. He explained to me that it was church—a place where men who wanted something different in their lives could come. I asked if I could join, and he refused me. One hundred men were already on the waiting list to come to a chapel with a seating capacity of one hundred.

I settled for his "No" answer that day because, after all, what point was there in wanting "something different" in a life like mine? My community, judges, prosecutors, probation, parole, and DOC—even some of my friends and family—had all stuck me with labels. And I'd bought into it.

But God made a way where there seemed to be no way. A short time later, I asked again for a seat in the chapel. To my surprise, the chaplain's answer was, "I don't know why I'm doing this, but I have a seat. In fact, I have two seats open—one on Sunday afternoon and one Monday night." Someone must've died or gone to ad seg (the hole) in order for that seat to be open. Their misfortune became my fortune.

They were playing the music again the day I attended my first chapel service. A man by the name of Jack Baize also shared God's Word. That Word (alive and powerful) convicted me of the horrible person I had become and the life I had settled for. He said that my life was valuable to God and that God loves me. Jack then testified that he had given his life to Jesus in a federal prison some twenty years earlier. Hearing him say that sparked hope in my heart for the first time in over thirty years, because at that point I couldn't stay out of prison more than ninety days.

He had been out twenty years. I wanted that. I needed that. That spark of hope in me became a big fire. I got on my knees at that little makeshift altar at JCCC. David said in Psalm 50:15, *Call upon Me in the day of trouble; I will deliver you, and you will honor Me.* I cried out to God and asked Him to change me.

And He did. I left the liar, thief, drug addict, dope dealer, con man, and master manipulator at the altar. *Therefore, if anyone is in Christ, he is a new creation; old things have passed away; behold, all things have become new* (2 Corinthians 5:17). I didn't get a better *old* life; I got a brand-new life. The Department of Corrections did not rehabilitate me. I wasn't reeducated, and I wasn't reformed. I was recreated by the King of

Kings and the Lord Himself. Jesus Christ is the hero of my story. At one o'clock, I entered the chapel a hopeless, broken, and lost man. I left at three o'clock, full of joy, love, peace, and hope. My old nickname in prison was, "The Crazy Cable Man". Within a month, they were calling me, "The Happy Convict". God poured so much love and joy into me, it oozed out. I couldn't contain it.

I had not yet been to trial on the armed-robbery case, but in August 2007 I went to trial in Cooper County on a change of venue from Pettis County. I was found guilty and went back in September and received a thirty-year-enhanced sentence. Because of all my prior felonies, I was starting a thirty-year sentence at age fifty. That meant I wouldn't be eligible for parole before age eighty. I was in a heap of trouble. But I want you to know, God reads a man's heart. The first thing I did when I got back to JCCC, was go to my knees. "So be it," I told God. "If this is where you want Johnny Allen to spend the rest of his life, I will do it serving you."

By the grace of God, I did not have to find out if I could live up to that statement. My armed-robbery case was presented to the Western District Appellate Court in Kansas City. In late 2009, my conviction was reversed. I won't go into all the details, but at the time of my arrest I had fourteen other charges pending and waiting for prosecution—charges like manufacturing within one-thousand feet of a school, possession, and distribution in the same location. All were twenty-year sentences that carry an 85% commitment. Burglaries, stealing, bad checks, and assault charges were all part of it. I was 100% guilty of all fourteen charges. By all rights, I should still be in prison today. My life had been insane.

But all charges were dropped in lieu of the big one—the robbery wasn't mine. God is good.

Much happened while I was in doing my last bit. My dad died. My youngest grandson was born. My youngest daughter married. Both my twin daughters experienced serious health issues. And my son and his family grew up, and over time grew distant. These are major events in a person's life; they're hurtful. Let me tell you, I didn't know how to handle it all; I was a baby Christian.

But one thing I didn't do; I didn't run to the yard looking for a dope sack to cover up my feelings. God has given me the strength, through Christ, to face my feelings and deal with them in a positive way.

Titus 3:3–5 says, *For we ourselves were once foolish, disobedient, led astray, slaves to various passions and pleasures, passing our days in malice and envy, hated by others and hating one another. But when the goodness and loving kindness of God our Savior appeared, he saved us, not because of works . . . but according to his own mercy.* Johnny Allen has experienced the goodness of God, His grace, His mercy, His love, and His forgiveness. When Jesus comes on the scene and the goodness and loving kindness of our Savior appears, hope comes alive.

I physically left the confinement of a maximum-security prison for the last time on March 21, 2011. But February 24, 2007—the lowest point in my life—was the day I gained my freedom. The things of the world that had attached themselves to me and me to them have been severed. I'm no longer bound by drugs, pornography, and criminal behavior. I'm not a burden to my family, my friends, the community, the courts, jails, and prisons. At the time of this writing, I've been clean fourteen years—four inside the walls and ten outside—and He's giving me energy to keep moving forward. He whom the Son sets free is free indeed (John 8:36).

In the past, I was considered a lost cause. But God gave me a new identity through His Son, Jesus. Grace rewrote my story. Jesus signed my pardon; my name is registered in heaven. I've gone from a prison cell to a guaranteed mansion.

Because my mind has been renewed, I'm capable of making better decisions. My family, in its entirety, has been restored. I do prison ministry, work in a Men's Christian Life program, serve in my church, and in my community. God is so good!

I'm telling you right now, don't quit; don't give up. If you quit, you end up back where you started. I did that too many times. Be desperate for a new life. Keep going; you're worth it. Make the comeback stronger than the setback.

I'm so in love with Jesus. Everything I was looking for in the world, I found in Him. I am His. He is mine. My prayer is that you will fall in love with Him as well. Jesus is waiting on you to run into His open arms. It is there that you will find peace regarding your past, a purpose for today, and a very-real hope for the future. God bless you dear friends!

Contact Information:
Johnny Allen
PO Box 64
Warsaw MO 65355
jlallensr30@gmail.com

KRAIZY

SHANA IKENBERRY

KRAIZY (CRAZY) WAS MY NICKNAME. Everyone called me that because I was the first one in—the one people called to do a job no one else would do. Although I was fourteen and the youngest of the crowd, I figured I knew it all.

My Father had been in prison since I was two years old, so I was raised by my stepdad and Mom. He was a workaholic, alcoholic. Not abusive—a happy drunk. Just never there. Because my mom wasn't a drinker, she became bored and lonely with him working all the time. So, she started hanging around the wrong people and doing drugs. On weekdays, I had to kick her friends out of the bathroom so I could get ready for school. I remember the sink spattered with blood, (at first, I didn't know it was from them shooting up). Since members of my family were addicts, this seemed normal. This lifestyle continued until my mom and stepdad went through a bad separation and divorce. They didn't realize the effect it had on us kids.

At age fourteen, I moved in with an older guy. He was a drug dealer. Always carried around a tacklebox with any kind of pill or drug a person could ever want. I was intrigued with the power it gave him over people. So, I used the drugs to manipulate others. I did drugs myself here and there, but mostly I was high on the control.

We would get kilos of cocaine from Wichita and rock it and triple our money. There was also a guy who supplied us with hundreds and hundreds of different pills. So, drugs were in abundance. We sold anything we could make a profit on. Back then, it was easier to get drugs than cigarettes or alcohol.

My boyfriend and I had a bad car wreck. That led me into a very toxic relationship with pain medicine. Opiates were like happiness in pill form . . . or so I thought.

About a year later, we were pulled over carrying a half-ounce of weighed and bagged cocaine. Being a minor, it was expected of me to take the charges. So, my charge was distribution of cocaine. I found out in court that we had been under surveillance for a year. Because of all the trouble I'd been in, the lawyer convinced my mom to sign me over to state's custody. I was sent to a maximum juvenile facility for two years. It was coed. All the walls were of glass, so you could see each other's rooms. I felt exposed, stripped of my independence and the power drugs had brought me. This was the first of my many jail and prison stays.

When I was released, I thought life would be great. It was too late; I was already addicted to prescription opiates. They were all I could think of. Because I believed them to be the answer to every problem, I continued letting them rule my life when I moved to Augusta. I managed to get three and sometimes four doctors at the same time to prescribe this medicine. With a super high tolerance to drugs, twenty Lortab 10's a day was what I needed to maintain. If I couldn't get them, I went to emergency rooms.

I'm not sure how the doctors found out about each other giving me the same script, but they all cut me off cold turkey. So, I resorted to drinking and buying drugs off the street. I used anything I could to lessen the physical and mental pain of withdrawal. Meth was cheaper, so I mixed Meth and Opiates. My life was miserable.

Since pills were expensive, I started doing bad things and hanging around bad people to obtain the drugs I thought I needed. Over the next fifteen years, I was constantly searching for love and happiness. I started dating the worst-of-the-worst type men. Dealers most of them. Scary men specializing in torture and collections. I heard screams and saw things that would traumatize most people. At this point, I was shooting a teener of meth every three days, doing handfuls of pills, and thought life was great.

Every time I split up with a boyfriend, I got drugs however I could. Robbing dope dealers was my favorite. My sick mind would justify it because they couldn't call the police. Right? A guy would scope it out inside and tell us where the guns and the big stash were. I'd then knock on the door—you know, with the special drug knock. When they answered, we'd rush in and take everything. I was especially addicted to the rush of being on the frontlines of death, always facing the possibility that something could go wrong.

Eventually, I got tired of being sick and tired. Every day, my only purpose in life was the next high.

I had just been questioned by the ATF for guns when someone knocked at my door. When I answered it, a guy was standing there holding a puppy. He said he was my real father and had just got out of prison in Wyoming. I hadn't seen him since I was two years old. So, I jumped in his truck and we headed out of state to my grandma's. I was able to spend about two weeks with him before the night he left me at a bar, promising to come right back. He never came; he died in a car wreck.

I had an eight-month-old son at the time—beautiful, and happy, such an amazing baby. My dad's unexpected death gave me a reason to twist off out of control and do the only things I knew—drugs, guns, and danger. Every day I woke up and drugged or drank until I passed out.

I always justified my behavior by blaming others. It was my mom's fault; it was my biological dad's fault. Poor me, poor me. I told myself that my son was better off without me. My grandparents would take good care of him.

Shame ate at me. Day after day, I chose drugs and men who used me and beat me. I blamed them and thought, *I can't bring my baby into this!* But I continued choosing drugs. Because I was in and out of jail, my grandparents took me to court for my son. This was the worst abandonment I had ever felt. They were my rock. That year, I lost my dad, my son, *and* my grandparents.

Four years later, I met a man who became my best friend. He and I ran hard together until I got pregnant. My little girl was so sweet and happy. So perfect. With this little one, I was going to do better; I was older and was going to *be* better.

The problem was, I had no idea what being better meant. The cycle continued. Several charges later, I gave birth to another perfect baby girl. She was so pretty; she laughed with her eyes. I ended up in jail for fourteen months. The girls' dad—my best friend—took care of them. But because he was active in addiction, my sister-in-law had to step in.

When I was released, there was nothing stopping me—no boyfriend, no kids. Only a hole in my heart that needed filling. And feelings of shame . . . Why couldn't I get it together? I searched for ways to numb the pain I had brought on myself. Being bad was the only thing I knew how to do well. So, I used that as my excuse for another toxic boyfriend, another robbery, more drugs, guns, gambling, more crazy, near-death experiences—just for the sake of feeling something. I wasn't afraid to die. I did and saw things I can never talk about. I also did so much dope I should have died many times. Still, I couldn't shake my sense of worthlessness—I figured I deserved to feel this way. What kind of mother abandons her children? I'd always thought *I'll just go party for a couple of days.* Those days turned into weeks, which turned into thirteen years away from my kids. I didn't want to live. I begged God to take me.

That's when it happened. God heard my cry. Prison. Four years. I thought my life was over. The withdrawal was horrendous. Feelings and emotions—I didn't even know I had—surfaced. I hated myself, everyone, and everything. Especially myself. *You deserve this!* was what I told myself when I cried myself to sleep every night.

But my mind began to clear. For the first time in my life, I didn't have to worry about a man beating me or a drug dealer retaliating. I started going to every callout and Christian service there was. I had asked Jesus into my heart as a child while sitting in the second row at church with my grandparents. But He was only a character in a book, a felt-board story in Sunday school. I didn't think Christianity worked for me.

One evening at a Christian callout, I felt something. What was it? Surely, this Christian stuff was fake. My grandparents took my son. They were supposed to be Christians and they hurt me badly. I didn't want anything to do with their God. This Savior, well where was He when I needed saving? when my kids needed saving? I was too far gone. *Unsavable* is what I told myself.

But I went up for prayer anyway and was filled with the Holy Spirit. By the time I made it back to my bunk, doubts had already resurrected. This hope and forgiveness were nothing but a fairy tale.

The next day I woke up feeling tingly, with a rush of happiness I had never felt before. No more mad, sad, and grumpy. The mean, hateful expression on my face was gone. I had a peace I could not explain or understand. Did this happen in every religious call out? I needed to know. For a while, I checked out other religions. But that peace wasn't there. Nor the power.

That's when I knew there was a change. This whole Jesus thing was real. I'd finally found the hope I was needing.

I started digging into the Word and Jesus began revealing His love for me. The way I thought and acted began to change. My heart was softening. Later, a lady told me she'd spent a year and a half with me in county jail. I didn't remember her, so I asked why we never talked. She said I was unapproachable, 'Kraizy'. That hit me hard. So, I asked God to continue changing my heart so I could love and be loved.

One night in my room, while crying about my kids and praying they'd forgive me and someday love me, I heard an audible voice. "If you stay faithful to Me, I will stay faithful and restore your family." Was I going crazy? Did I really hear that? I knew deep in my spirit, it was real.

While I was in prison, I heard about a place called Working Men of Christ (WMOC). My mind wasn't renewed yet, so I saw this place as a hustle, a way to get back to my hometown and my mom.

When I got out, I went to WMOC House of Esther. The people believed in me; they loved me—not the world's kind of love, or the what-can-you-do-for-me love. It was different and genuine. I started learning the principles and promises of the Bible and who God called me to be. I was created for so much more. God gave me my name back. I am no longer *Kraizy*. I am Shannah and I have been called for a greater purpose.

After a year there, I moved on to Katie Souza's ministry for eight months. That's where I started seeing God's power—miracles, signs, and wonders. She taught me how to get my soul healed. Wow, what a revelation! Let me tell you something. Just being a Christian is not enough; you must work on your soul. Throughout my life there was such sin and trauma, rejection, abandonment, you name it. So, I started learning the steps to freedom.

When I returned to WMOC, I walked it out. There, they showed me how to deal with everyday situations in a godly manner. I was getting my soul healed as I continued to surrender in obedience to the call of God on my life. The craving for drugs, guns, and danger fell away. It didn't happen overnight or even in my timing, but I felt free. I knew my calling, my purpose, my passion was to help others come out of a life of *kraizyness*. God started giving me back everything the devil stole.

After four years, I got the call from my sister-in-law. She said the girls were wanting to meet me. I lost it. Fear flooded me. I didn't know how to be a mom. I feared rejection. Was I worthy of them even knowing me? Wouldn't they be better off without me? This went on in my head like a whirlwind. I'd no more cast one thought down and another would come.

We set up a time to meet my girls first. I felt such happiness. They were so beautiful. If only I could now see my son . . . We all met the next day in a restaurant. He and his sisters had never met. I was in complete awe. My tears flowed, not just because we were together for the first time (though that was the best thing ever), but because the Maker of heaven and earth remembered His promise to me. This was a miracle.

My kids still struggle with understanding why I was selfish and chose drugs and alcohol over them. But now I can explain to them about the soul wounds that governed me and how through sin and trauma I was lost . . . but God. We are working on our feelings and on understanding each other's feelings. And forgiveness. I can't take the past back, but I can make the future better. I know that me getting my soul healed will help save our family from generational stuff passed down. I am a work in progress as I sacrifice and surrender daily.

I am almost ten-years sober. I have an amazing job with WMOC, helping women who have gone through the same things I have. I also go into prisons and tell inmates, "If God can forgive and help me—the worst of the worst, the *Kraziest*, the most unlovable—then you too can be forgiven and restored to your family." I remind them of those promises in the Bible. They are ours, our inheritance. Stand on them and watch Him work. Be faithful to Him and the call, and I promise He will be faithful and honor those promises.

I'm also a KDOC badged mentor, and a chaplain at a county jail, where I have a key and can come and go as I please. That is so God! I have not only seen miracles, signs, and wonders, I expect them. It has become my norm.

So, that's my story of how Kraizy was born and then died. My name is Shannah. I am the righteousness of Christ Jesus. I am above and not beneath. I am the head and not the tail. I am loved and can love. I have been called to call others. If you are reading this, then you my friend have also been called. Come out of the depression, the hopelessness. You were created for more. Someone out there is waiting for you to show them. If we can do it, they can do it! Dig deep into the Bible. Start building a relationship with God; learn about His character, His personality. Surround yourself with positive influences—a mentor, a pastor, a volunteer. Watch God work.

Contact Information:
Shannah Ikenberry
PO Box 47491
Wichita KS 67201

THE OVERLOOKED

MATT THOMAS

I was born in Oregon in 1977 to a father addicted to methamphetamines and whatever else was available. My mom was an alcoholic. Together, they made for poor influences as parents.

A few years later we moved to Nevada, where my dad got so whacked out that he started locking up my mom in the house. When she finally became fed up with his abuse, she and I moved to my aunt and uncle's. Living quarters were tight, but we were starting over. From there, we moved to the projects in Reno, where early mornings found my mom sitting in her rocking chair with a loaded pistol to ensure that no one broke into our apartment.

As my mom's drinking increased, my respect for her decreased. Though she spanked and disciplined me, I wouldn't listen. Out of hurt and anger, I refused to obey. As a single mom working two jobs, she was at her wit's end with her rebellious six year old.

She finally landed a higher paying job and moved us into a better neighborhood thinking that would change my behavior. It did not. After repeatedly stealing from a store built in a field I previously tried to burn, it was time to change locations again.

I was starting third grade when we moved into a house. That didn't change things either. Mom spent much of her time drinking and partying. Which left me having to spend nights at daycares and in her various drinking buddies' homes. On several occasions, I stayed with a family who had three sons. The boys took me into their closet and did things that should never be done to a young boy. I stuffed it all inside, knowing I wasn't allowed to say anything. Even if I could, what would I tell people?

This ate me up inside. Of course, being diagnosed with ADD didn't help matters any. I felt completely alone, not knowing how to explain what was happening. My dad wasn't around to help me. Neither could my mom's boyfriend help at this point. I was so angry and rebellious, I hated everything he and my mom did.

My stealing continued. I stole a pair of gloves one day. Because I got away with it, I returned later with a friend and stole more. That became our pattern until the Christmas Eve they caught us. While mom was home decorating our Christmas tree, I was getting arrested. I ended up in juvenile hall with two counts of grand larceny. In court, they fined me and put me on probation.

Another time, a fifth grader and I broke into our school. I wrapped my hand in a jacket and put my fist through the window to open the door just like I'd seen done on TV. While we were stealing money from the library, setting a fire, and vandalizing, police surrounded the building. They told us to come out with our hands up. Though it had been my idea, I blamed it on the older kid. They believed me. I ended up doing community service. After that, we moved to Los Angeles, California.

Moving didn't change the fact that I was a mess. By fifth grade I was warped from being abused and confused about sex—or for that matter, love at all. I had no understanding about intimate affection expressed in a loving context designed and approved by God. So, I fooled around with other kids, and even a cousin. I knew something about it wasn't right, but I was so hurt I didn't understand.

This continued until I was caught with another boy. When the parents tried to press charges, I told my mom about what happened when I was young. She kept saying, "Why didn't you tell me? Why didn't you tell me?" Dad, fresh out of prison, was trying to be in my life again. But he was drinking heavily and was strung out on methamphetamines and shooting heroin. He called me a "gay weirdo" because he didn't understand why I let it go on for so long. Today, I still deal with the pain and shame of my father putting all blame on me. It feels like hate, and love, and disgust all wrapped up in one. It tarnishes everything I do.

After I turned twelve, we moved to West Covina, California. My heart was full of sadness from the twisted activities that shaped my younger years. All I wanted was to be loved by my dad and to make him proud.

At age thirteen, he announced that I was a man. Therefore, like a man, I was going to drink with him. That started my journey with drinking, partying, smoking weed, and doing other drugs with him. My dad—with his tough guy, biker, drug addict image—was the coolest thing in the world. I wanted to be like him, so life became all about partying with him.

I really stepped into the drug lifestyle when we moved to Fullerton in Orange County. It was at my uncle's friend's house that I first tried meth. When the drug entered my system, the feeling was more than euphoria. I felt anger, and sadness, and every other emotional memory all mixed together. After all the pain, the drama, the *everything* in my life, I felt normal. I was going to be okay.

Then I came down. But I was already hooked. I stole everything of value from my mom to trade for drugs. Anything I owned, I sold to buy drugs. I was so addicted, so desperate, that one night I came close to shooting a friend over a case of beer.

I felt more like a creature than a whole person. An outcast. Forgotten. But when I was high, I felt alive. So, getting high was all that mattered.

I got my first tattoo at age thirteen. My dad also shot me up with heroin. He wanted me to try it at home, not on the street. It was my first and last time. In hindsight, God used that experience to keep me away from intravenous drugs—heroin in particular.

By age fourteen, I was messing up really bad. My mom was forced to hide everything of value and get rid of her gun so I couldn't use it. She was a full-blown alcoholic by then, living with a raging drug addict. Those were not good times in our lives. It was time to get sober, so she checked herself into rehab. It was probably the best thing that could've ever happened to us. The positive thing about struggles and troubles, is that there's this thing called collateral beauty, (although many times you can't see the beauty until you're older). But all this craziness shapes you into who God wants you to be. It's just hard to see it when you're in the moment.

I went through high school with a serious drug addiction. I was super skinny, dropping acid because it was so cheap, smoking marijuana, and doing speed (or meth). Because I had no credits and a less-than-F average grade, dropping out of school seemed the logical move. Mom sent me to a school for wayward boys.

The Independent Fundamental Baptist School had extremely strict standards. They believed in the King James Version Bible only. Women were to wear dresses only, and no music but hymns were accepted. Talk about a culture shock! But they showed me how to work, and I loved it. They also showed me who Jesus was, though at the time all I could see was the legalistic side—the don't do this, don't do that—and I missed having a relationship with Jesus or God.

I finally graduated high school, but college was a different matter. I didn't know how to study, how to hold down a job, or live a real life. I didn't know how to be a man. So, I returned to partying, getting high, and having fun. It was what I knew. I ended up living with an aunt in Vegas, selling magazines door to door. Through this, I met a girl and got her pregnant. When she joined the crew to be with me, they separated us. So, we moved in with my mom in Long Beach.

Because I was going to be a father, I needed a job. I joined the Navy and became a sonar technician on a submarine. For the first time in my life, I did well. However, I wasn't done with drugs. I started getting high again. So did my wife. Before long, I was selling drugs to others in my division, making enough to support my habit and still make a few bucks.

Things went downhill fast. Long story short, we became full-blown addicts and split up. I ended up with an honorable discharge I didn't deserve and me and the kids moved to Washington. All I did was get high and take care of them. Nine months later, my ex-wife showed, claiming she wanted to work things out. We moved to Arizona. It turned out to be a scheme to get her kids back. And it worked. I ended up alone and homeless.

By this time, I was down to smoking marijuana only, convinced that it wasn't a drug. I did cocaine one night and that led me back to my drug of choice—meth.

I got a job at a brake shop. We worked all day, and at night ran stolen cars through. When we ran out of drugs, our manager used the shop's deposit to keep us high, claiming the money was stolen.

I married another drug addict and continued spiraling downhill. While this wife was calling me a piece of garbage, my ex was telling me to come get my kids or she'd tie them to a tree. At this same time, my wife's friend introduced me to spiritual things. Random spiritual experiences began to happen. One was at a bus stop when I struck up a conversation with a stranger who looked like a tweaker. When he handed me some meth and said, 'Here you go, Matt', I noticed for the first time his totally black eyes—no white, no color to them. It freaked me out. I got on a bus and left, taking the drugs with me.

In 2002, I spent three months in a Salvation Army rehab in Tucson. It was the longest I'd been clean and sober in some time. I was in good shape, even spent time with my children and mom. Later that year, my ex-wife took the girls to Kansas and I didn't hear from her again for a long time.

I blew my sobriety when I moved back to Arizona and reconnected with the woman who introduced me to the spiritual realm. Strange spiritual experiences increased. Once, when she talked to me, it was as though someone else was speaking through her. She never blinked. It was the weirdest thing. Another time, I dreamed about a giant dog. I knew it represented evil. And it wanted me. Later on, at her house, she described the whole dream to me.

When I found out my dad died from being beaten, everything changed for the worse. My using and selling drugs got out of control. I robbed people, broke into homes, stole cars and trailers, and kicked with a group of criminals operating on a higher level.

But there's no honor among thieves even at that level. I came to find out that my name was involved in all thefts, drug dealing, armed robberies, and trafficking. They even robbed cartels, using my name so I'd get killed. I never saw it. I ended up getting arrested a number of times, but the charges never stuck.

A couple months before I went to court again on one of the charges, I met Christina. She was an addict, not a criminal. I turned her into a career criminal. In the middle of everything, I got arrested and was sentenced with three years in prison. Looking back on things, I realize that the hand of God was moving in my life on many occasions, though I didn't have eyes to see it yet.

As I was mentally preparing for prison, I ran into my old dealer, Steve. He gave me some solid advice. Do your prison time, get out, be a man, and raise your children. Don't waste time with drugs and the drug lifestyle.

I was still processing what Steve said when I arrived at Apache Unit, Winslow State Prison. The norm for prison is extortion and pride, anger and racism, hatred, and drug abuse—everything that put me there in the first place. But I was hungry. All I wanted was to know God, to feel and experience Him. So, I stuck my nose in the Bible.

Arizona prisons are extremely segregated. One didn't bunk or mix with another race unless you were looking for a fight. Another rule was, don't get caught stealing. One day while I was working in the kitchen, an inmate twice my size tried to get me to pass food through the slot. When I refused, he called me a punk and I knew I'd have to fight him. Back at the housing unit, I put on my boots and went into the closet with him. He looked at me and said, "Man, I don't want to fight you. I apologize." We shook hands and left it at that. I didn't realize yet that God was taking the hopelessness of this prison yard and doing something amazing with it.

God blessed that yard of four-hundred-and-forty inmates. The church we planted inside the walls grew to seventy-to-eighty people on Saturday nights. God honored our Friday night prayers and fasting. Soon, we were able to eat together, have cookouts with other races, and as a church do things we'd normally never get to do. The heads of the yard even showed up for our Christmas services.

I came out of prison on fire for God. Amazing things happened because of God's love and blessings on me. The second day out, I landed a great job in a restaurant, was working with good people. After that, I got another job.

Then I met a girl and instead of walking with God, I lived in sin with her. Let me just say that when you step out of God's will, you end up right back in the mess of problems He was protecting you from. My sobriety was blown. Though I never started drinking or getting high on meth or weed, I abused prescription meds.

Shortly after my parole in September 2009, someone brutally murdered my ex-wife. This destroyed my daughters, who were under my mom's care by then because of the abuse they'd experienced at the hand of their mother. Despite their pain, I was still wrapped up in my own life and wasn't able to step in and be their dad. I finally joined them in Kansas the end of 2010.

Of course, the girl I was with came with me. Although I wanted to be a dad to my kids, she hurt my daughters even more. So, back to Arizona she went, rather quickly.

A few months later, I reconnected (through social media) with Christina, my fiancé while I was in prison. Although we began our relationship slowly because of my history of treating women so badly, we did get back together. She ended up pregnant. A few months later, we almost lost the baby.

The day after the ER nurse told us there was little chance of our baby making it, I had a serious talk with God. "God, I understand I deserve this. I've spit in your face, disrespected you, and treated you like garbage. I've welched on everything I've ever told you, but I ask this one time, please don't let this baby die. I promise we will not have sex anymore till we are married." We kept our word and now have a beautiful boy named Hunter. He's more than a gift from God.

My pastor from Arizona performed our wedding ceremony in my mom's backyard. He drove all that way to make sure we were right with

God. Over the next few months, God felt really close, and I sought Him like never before. Everything in my life changed. I dug deeper into His Word, downloaded podcasts and sermons to listen to while I worked third-shift maintenance at a church. I knew there was a call on my life but didn't quite know what it was yet.

I felt God pulling me toward working with prisoners, though I didn't understand how to walk it out. When Christina and I saw a TV commercial about a program called Mentoring for Success in the Kansas prisons, I called them. I was told later that Mentoring for Success never makes commercials. It's a God mystery.

Because I was a five-time felon, I figured I'd never get approved to go in. I was petrified and on the verge of backing out when I mentioned my past to my trainer. He said, "Don't worry about it. You'll be fine. I promise you'll be okay." Two weeks later, I got the call to pick up my ID. I was good to go.

I go to prisons a lot now. The program started giving me trouble-makers to mentor because I too had been in prison. It was a blessing and at the same time frustrating because I couldn't figure out why they kept giving me these knuckleheads to help. I just wanted some nice-and-easy guy I could mentor. What I didn't understand was that God was preparing me to do this very thing for Him.

God started burdening me about re-entry and how these guys had nothing when released from prison. When I asked at church why we didn't have a prison ministry, the answer was, "Because you haven't started one yet, Matt."

God gave me a vision for a ministry similar to the one I went through when released from prison in Arizona. Firm Foundation Ministries was birthed. What began as one place for men to stay when leaving prison, has now grown to three homes in Wichita KS, one opening soon in Kansas City KS, and one in Topeka KS.

While in the process of opening these re-entry homes, I got to preach my first sermon in El Dorado Prison. It was a short five minutes, but powerful. After that, I started speaking at Hutchinson Correctional Facility, where we later planted two churches, one in medium and one in minimum. The prison church plants are successful because of the empowered men still behind bars.

About a year into it, the subject of Lansing Prison came up in a phone conversation between a buddy and me. Since Lansing is the biggest prison in the state of Kansas, we naturally thought it should be our next target of concentration.

Six months later, while I was interviewing guys in Lansing's Brothers in Blue Re-Entry Program who had applied to come into our program, their director resigned. Someone suggested I apply for the position. "Well, certain things would have to happen for me to even try," I answered. Wouldn't you know, those things happened.

So, I applied. Not getting the job led me down a path of uncertainty as to my calling and a month of quasi-depression. I kept asking myself, *what am I doing wrong? Why would God set this up and not let it happen?*

A month later I got a phone call that forever changed my life. "Hi Matt! We want you to be part of the team of Brothers in Blue Re-Entry and run the program portion of our ministry." I wanted it too. Although I felt unqualified to manage this giant program, I knew God wanted me there. I moved to Kansas City to start work right away. Within two weeks, our house in Wichita sold for cash money and my family joined me.

There are different ways of viewing prisons. One is from the prisoner's perspective. Visitors have their perspective. Then there's the contract staff's perspective. Working forty-plus hours a week—watching and studying other people and other organizations, seeing how churches interact and visit—gave me better insight and understanding into the hurts and pains of the system. God gave me a burden and a vision of how to work together to build a model that is efficient and reproducible. As a church, we are missing a giant community of people. If someone is a violent offender, a sex offender, a snitch, or any other thing people put a jacket on, then that person has a tough road ahead. If we want to see revival, we need to be trained and prepared for it with church plants inside prisons, and people discipled in how to walk with prisoners once they are released.

True change begins with the heart. That change comes only through salvation in Christ. The amazing thing about God, is that He intentionally shows us that, and through showing gives us purpose, and direction. He also shows us that there is something greater than ourselves out there. God designed a great life for convicted felons, even after incarceration. He is bigger than our surroundings, bigger than our situations, greater than our struggles. This is true. I have seen it in my own life.

Read Matt's whole story in his book: *The Overlooked.*

Contact Information:
Matt Thomas
Firm Foundations
PO Box 8628
Wichita, KS 67208
matthomas01@gmail.com

RESOURCES FOR BIBLE STUDIES

Below are some places you can write to and request a Bible correspondence course to help you grow in your faith.

- WORKING MEN OF CHRIST
  PO Box 47491
  Wichita KS 67201
- AMERICAN BIBLE ACADEMY
  PO Box 1627
  Joplin MO 64802-1627
- CLI PRISON ALLIANCE
  4754 Hargrove Rd Suite 100
  Raleigh NC 27616

YOU CAN HAVE "THE REAL THING"

"The Real Thing" has nothing to do with "religion."

Rather, it is an intimate personal relationship with our Heavenly Father, because of the finished work of Jesus at the Cross. The Holy Spirit comes and seals us as His very own, and begins an ongoing work in us to conform us to the image of Christ Jesus.

You can begin this exciting and abundant life today. It will continue throughout all eternity.

First, acknowledge and confess that you have sinned against God.

Second, renounce your sins – determine that you are not going back to them. Turn away from sin. Turn to God.

Third, by faith receive Christ into your heart. Surrender your life completely to Him. He will come to live in your heart by the Holy Spirit.

You can do this right now.

Start by simply talking to God. You can pray a prayer like this:

"Oh God, I am a sinner. I'm sorry for my sin. I want to turn from my sin. Please forgive me . I believe Jesus Christ is Your Son; I believe He died on the Cross for my sin and You raised Him to life. I want to trust Him as my Savior and follow Him as my Lord from this day forward, forevermore. Lord Jesus, I put my trust in You and surrender my life to You. Please come into my life and fill me with your Holy Spirit. In Jesus' Name. Amen."

If you just said this prayer, and you meant it with all your heart, we believe you just got Saved and are now Born Again in Christ Jesus as a totally new person.

"Therefore, if anyone is in Christ, he is a new creation; the old has gone, the new has come!" (II Corinthians 5:17)

We urge you to go "all in and all out for the All in All"! (Pastor Mark Batterson, *All In*)

We suggest you follow the Lord in water baptism at your earliest opportunity. Water baptism is an outward symbol of the inward change that follows your salvation and re-birth.

The grace of God Himself gives you the desire and ability to surrender completely to the Holy Spirit's work in and through you (Philippians 2:13).

The Baptism in the Holy Spirit is His empowerment for you.

YOU CAN RECEIVE THE BAPTISM IN THE HOLY SPIRIT

The Baptism in the Holy Spirit is a separate experience and a Holy privilege granted to those who ask. This is God's own power to enable you to live an abundant, overcoming life. The Bible says it is the same power that raised Jesus from the dead (Romans 1:4; 8:11; II Cor. 4:13-14; 1 Peter 3:18).

Have you asked the Father for Jesus to baptize you (immerse you) in the Holy Spirit (Luke 3:16)? If you ask the Father, He will give Him to you (Luke 11:1). Have you allowed the "rivers of living water" to flow from within you (John 7:38-39)? Our Father desires for us to walk in all His fullness by His Holy Spirit.

The power to witness, and live your life the way Jesus did in intimate relationship with the Father, comes from asking Jesus to baptize you in the Holy Spirit. To receive this baptism, pray along these lines:

Abba Father and my Lord Jesus,

Thank you for giving me your Spirit to live inside me. I am saved by grace through faith in Jesus. I ask you now to baptize me in the Holy Ghost with Your fire and power. I fully receive it through faith just like I did my salvation. Now, Holy Spirit, come and rise up within me as I praise God! Fill me up Jesus! I fully expect to receive my prayer language as You give me utterance. In Jesus' Name. Amen.

Now, out loud, begin to praise and glorify JESUS, because He is the baptizer of the Holy Spirit! From deep in your spirit, tell Him, "I love you, I thank you, I praise you, Jesus."

Repeat this as you feel joy and gratefulness bubble up from deep inside you. Speak those words and syllables you receive – not in your own language, but the heavenly language given to you by the Holy Spirit. Allow this joy to come out of you in syllables of a language your own mind does not already know. That will be your prayer language the Spirit will use through you when you don't know how to pray (Romans 8:26-28). It is not the "gift of tongues" for public use, therefore it does not require a public interpretation.

You have to surrender and use your own vocal chords to verbally express your new prayer language. The Holy Spirit is a gentleman. He will not force you to speak. Don't be concerned with how it sounds. It is a heavenly language!

Worship Him! Praise Him! Use your heavenly language by praying in the Spirit every day! Paul urges us to "pray in the Spirit on all occasions with all kinds of prayers and requests." (Ephesians 6:18)